A Rare Night Indeed

by A.L. Sullivan

Dedicated to:

Brooke Lynn
and
Jennifer Paige

Birthday Spooks

Rare
Night
Indeed

It's Halloween
so come with me
I'll show you
the tricks of the trade.

We'll walk alone,
in dark streets unknown,
if we're lucky,
we might see a shade.

For all Hallows Eve,
is a rare night indeed,
When spirits are free
to roam.

Wherever they choose,
they have nothing to lose,
They may even
enter your home.

So let's go out,
scream and shout,
Dress 'n prepped in
our guise.

A sneak and a grin,
we'll fit right in,
Then show them our
ghoulish surprise.

We'll walk all night,
cause such fright,
As we howl at the
bright yellow moon.

We'll jump and run,
have such fun,
We may wake the dead
from their tombs.

As we roam around town,
we will go down,
To random houses
on the street.

When they open the door,
we'll let out a roar,
'n shriek
"Trick or Treat!"

The End

Riddles N' Rhymes, Fun Times

1. "ee's" for eyes, he sees you from out his pumpkin shell. On which pages is he? Can you tell?

2. "Whoo R U Now" is written hidden high on a page. Can you figure out where it lays?

3. That "ee" eyed pumpkin once got shrunk, can you find that little, sneaky, punk?

4. Which page, when turned to the opposite angle, reveals faces opposite their other faces dangle.?

5. "ee" eyed pumpkin feel his gaze, from all, except, which one page?

6. We mark the grave with a stone, on which initials are shown?

7. Stars on her sorcerous hat. Where is that pretty princess at?

8. Spooky cats appear next to each other, one cheshire, looking nothing like the other.

9. Mini Monkey Maze, to the X encircled in his tongue. Make your way from the S, then you are done.

10. Have you seen "The Last Page", the real last page?

Riddle Answers

1. Page 4,6,8,10, 14, 16, 20, 22, the end.

2. Page 12 Top right corner (in spiky branch).

3. Page 10 Bottom left (peeking between the porch bars).

4. Page 16 Faces upside-up and upside down.

5. Page 12 No "ee" eyed pumpkin.

6. Page 18 JVA on the headstone (bottom right corner).

7. Page 22 Merlin hat, princess with necklace and hair in a bun. (Left Top Quadrant).

8. Page 8 Cheshire with missing teeth and (face only) Whiskers (right bottom quadrant).

9. Page 20 Maze, bottom right corner "S" is the start, "X" marks the finish.

10. Turn the page for "The Last Page" a poem, also by Alysa Lynn Peters

The Last Page

Sad 'n lonely it sits,
it's words the last to be read.
Locked away in darkness,
it's words so full of dread.
For the last page brings an ending,
be it good or bad.
The last page brings silence,
full, still and sad.

\- A.L. Sullivan

About the Author

Amanda Sullivan is a Utah based author, artist and poet. Amanda writes poetry and children's books, from halloween coloring books to alphabet poetry books. Amanda is a wife and mother of 4 bright souls whom she claims are the inspiration for her poetry, art, and music. Amanda has been inspired by the rhythm of poetry from a young age. Among her favorite poets are: Edgar Allen Poe, Robert Frost, and Dr Seuss.

Amanda studied poetry throughout high school in Star Valley, Wyoming. She took classes at Northwest College in Powell, Wyoming and continues discovering poetry everyday. Just like most children, Amanda loved to doodle and draw as a child. Amanda continued doodle-ing and creating art throughout her life. Those doodles evolved into the complex "drawings" you see in her works today! Her black and white abstract art in her Halloween children's coloring book has inspired many children to use their imaginations as they color and fill in the white spaces.

Find more information about Amanda on Facebook.
Facebook.com/AuthorALSullivan